Capitol kids!
Hits

Today's Biggest Christian Radio Hits

Arranged for kids by Brian Hitt

Available Products:

www.brentwoodbenson.com
www.starsong.com

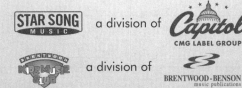

STAR SONG MUSIC — a division of **Capitol** CMG LABEL GROUP

KIDZ MUSIC CLUB — a division of **BRENTWOOD-BENSON** music publications

Contents

Advanced Choir Specials

God's Not Dead (Like a Lion)

Words and Music by
DANIEL BASHTA
Arranged by Brian Hitt

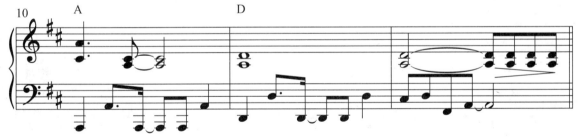

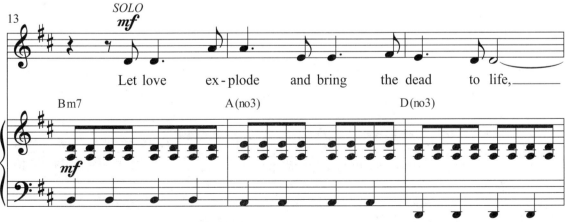

Let love ex-plode and bring the dead to life,____

4

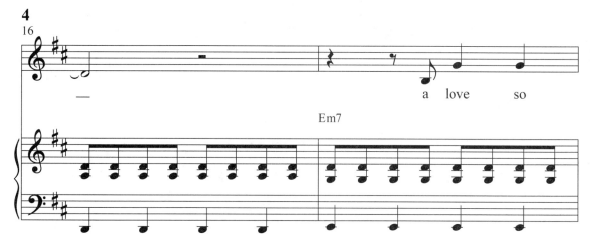

a love so

Em7

ALL   *SOLO*

bold   to see a rev-o-lu - tion   some - how.

Bm7   G2

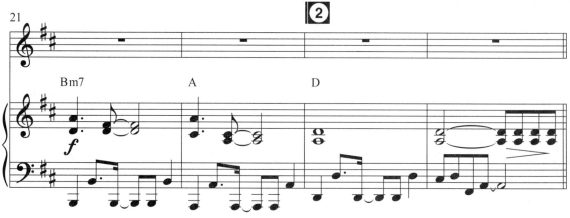

②

Bm7   A   D

f

mf

Let love   ex-plode   and bring   the dead   to life,_____

Bm7   A   D

mf

Gold

Words and Music by
BRITT NICOLE, DAN MUCKALA
and JESS CATES
Arranged by Brian Hitt

Oh, oh, oh, oh oh oh.___

SMALL GROUP

You're go - o - o - o - old.___

D♭   Fm

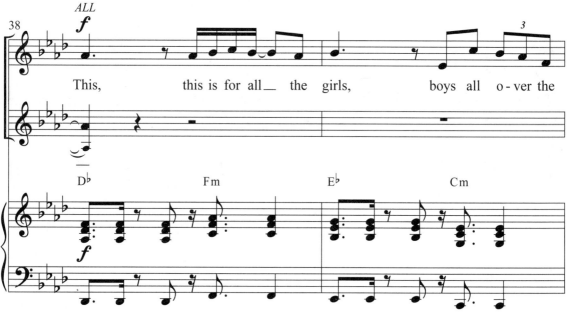

ALL
f

This,   this is for all__ the girls,   boys all o - ver the

D♭   Fm   E♭   Cm

f

world.   What-ev-er you've been told,   you're worth more than gold.

D♭   Fm   E♭   Cm

We Believe

Words and Music by
MATTHEW HOOPER, RICHIE FIKE
and TRAVIS RYAN
Arranged by Brian Hitt

In this time of des-per-a-tion

when all we know is doubt and fear,

24

There is on - ly___ one sal - va - tion:___ We be-lieve,

___ we be-lieve. We be-lieve

___ in__ God the Fa - ther, we be-lieve___ in__ Je-sus Christ, we be - lieve

___ in the Ho - ly Spir - it, and He's giv-en us___ new life. We be-lieve

53
_____ Your love will nev-er fail! We be-lieve,_____ we be-lieve!_____ We be-lieve

55
_____ in God the Fa - ther, we be-lieve_____ in Je-sus Christ, we be-lieve

57
_____ in the Ho-ly Spir - it,_____ and He's giv-en us_____ new life. We be-lieve

59
_____ in the cru-ci-fix - ion, we be-lieve_____ that He con-quered death, we be-lieve

Me Without You

Words and Music by
TOBY McKEEHAN, DAVID GARCIA
and CHRIS STEVENS
Arranged by Brian Hitt

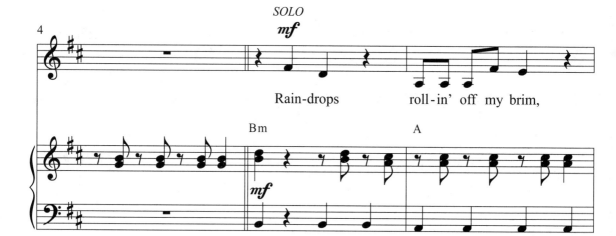

We Are Brave!

Words and Music by
CHRIS STEVENS, DAVID GARCIA
and SHAWN MCDONALD
Arranged by Brian Hitt

We got style, we got grace, and we walk it___ bold.

We got hearts full of life that are made out of gold.

We're a-live, we're a-live and we keep on mov-

in', mov-in'.

31 *2nd time*

1. *(page 47, meas. 65)*

73

2.

SOLO (or SMALL GROUP)

in'.   Oo whoa oh oh   oh whoa oh._____   Oo

Am   Dm

76

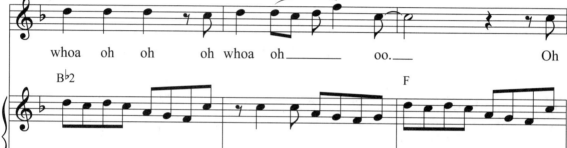

whoa oh oh   oh whoa oh_____   oo.__   Oh

B♭2   F

79 **32**

ALL
f

whoa oh_____   oo.__   And we say

C

82

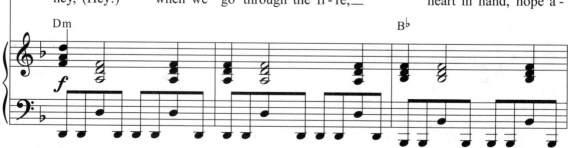

hey, (Hey!)   when we go through the fi-re,___   heart in hand, hope a-

Dm   B♭

f

live, it-'ll be o - kay.___ (Hey!) When we walk a-cross a wi-re,___

we___ won't back down 'cause we are brave.

___ (Hey!) when we go through the fi - re,___

SOLO

When we go through the fi -

I Am

Words and Music by
DAVID CROWDER and ED CASH
Arranged by Brian Hitt

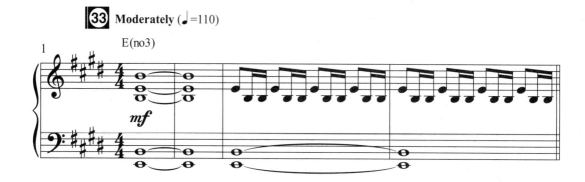

There's no space that His love can't reach.

There's no place where we can't find peace.

There's no end to a - maz - ing grace.

ALL *SOLO*

Take me in with Your

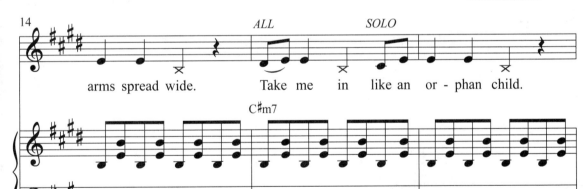

ALL *SOLO*

arms spread wide. Take me in like an or - phan child.

34

Nev-er let go, nev-er leave my side.____

mid-dle of __ this storm,   I am hold-ing on.   I___ am

_   hold-ing   on   to__ You.__   I___ am

E(no3)

_   hold-ing   on   to__ You.__   In the

C#m7

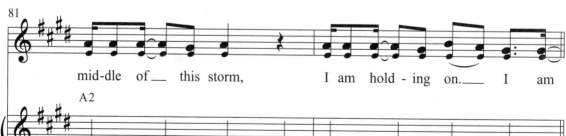

mid-dle of __ this storm,   I am hold-ing on.__   I am

A2

holding on to__ You.__ I am

holding on to__ You.__ In the

mid-dle of __ this storm I am hold-ing on, I am.

Oceans (Where Feet May Fail)

Words and Music by
JOEL HOUSTON, MATT CROCKER
and SALOMON LIGHTHELM
Arranged by Brian Hitt

the great un - known where feet may

_ fail._____ And there I

find You in the mys - t'ry, in o - ceans

_ deep my faith will__ stand._____

ALL

And I will call up-on__ Your

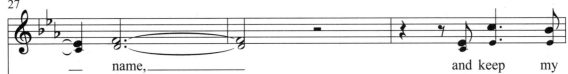

__ name,_____ and keep my

eyes a - bove the__ waves._____ When o - ceans

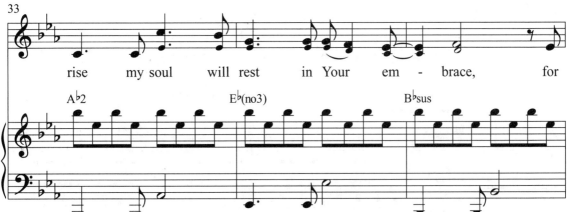

rise my soul will rest in Your em - brace, for

Where feet may fail and fear sur-rounds me,

You've nev - er___ failed and You won't___ start

_ now.___ So I will

call up-on___ Your___ name,___

call___ me. Take me deep - er than my feet

___ could ev - er wan - der, and my faith___ will be___ made strong-

- ger in the pres - ence of___ my Sav - ior.

I will call up-on___ Your___ name,_____

Waterfall

Words and Music by
CHRIS TOMLIN and ED CASH
Arranged by Brian Hitt

O God, my God I seek You, I wan-na move when You move. You're more than I could long for, I thirst for You. You're an o- could long for, I thirst for You. You're an o-

when I call, when I call, deep calls___ to deep.___

Your love is like a wa-ter-fall, wa-ter-fall,___ rain-ing down

___ on___ me.___

Wa - ter - fall, wa - ter - fall.

Write Your Story

Words and Music by
FRANCESCA BATTISTELLI,
BEN GLOVER and DAVID GARCIA
Arranged by Brian Hitt

sing,　　the Source of the rhy-thm my　heart　keeps　beat-ing.　They

_ say　You can give the blind their sight,　and You can bring the dead to

life,　You can be the hope my　soul's　been　seek-in'.　I

wan-na tell You now that I be-lieve it,　I wan-na tell You now that I be-lieve it, I_

39
on my heart; come on and make Your mark.____

41
Au-thor of my hope, Mak-er of the stars, let me be Your

43
work of art. Won't You write Your sto-ry on my heart?

45
Write Your sto-ry, write Your sto-ry, come on and

Au-thor of my hope, Mak-er of the stars, let me be Your

work of art. Won't You write Your sto-ry on my heart?

SMALL GROUP

Write Your sto-ry, write Your sto-ry, come on and

Speak Life

Words and Music by
TOBY McKEEHAN, JAMIE MOORE
and RYAN STEVENSON
Arranged by Brian Hitt

2nd time to ⊕
(page 97, meas. 33)

52

hope, You speak love, You speak. Speak

54

life,_____ oh_____ oh oh__ oh oh.__ Speak

SMALL GROUP

Speak life, speak life.

56

life,_____ oh_____ oh oh__ oh oh.__ You speak

Speak life, speak life.

This Is Amazing Grace

Words and Music by
PHIL WICKHAM, JOSH FARRO
and JEREMY RIDDLE
Arranged by Brian Hitt

that You would bear my__ cross.__

You__laid down Your life_____ that I would be set

free._____ Oh. Je-sus, I sing for

SMALL GROUP

Whoa_____ oh.__

Hello, My Name Is

Words and Music by
MATTHEW WEST
Arranged by Brian Hitt

30

for the ver - y___ last___ time.

Hel - lo, my name is child of the one true King.

___ I've been saved, I've been changed, I have been set___ free.

___ "A - maz - ing___ Grace"___ is the song I___ sing.

changed, I have been set free. "A - maz - ing Grace"

C♭2

is the song I sing. Hel - lo, my name is

A♭m7   C♭2

child of the one, true King. Whoa oh ah

G♭

122

Overcomer

Words and Music by
DAVID GARCIA, BEN GLOVER
and CHRIS STEVENS
Arranged by Brian Hitt

Ooo_____

I know He's not gon - na let_____ it get the best of you.__

ALL

You're an o - ver-com - er,_____ stay in the fight

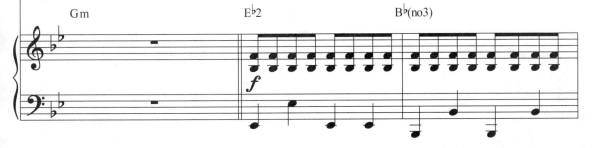

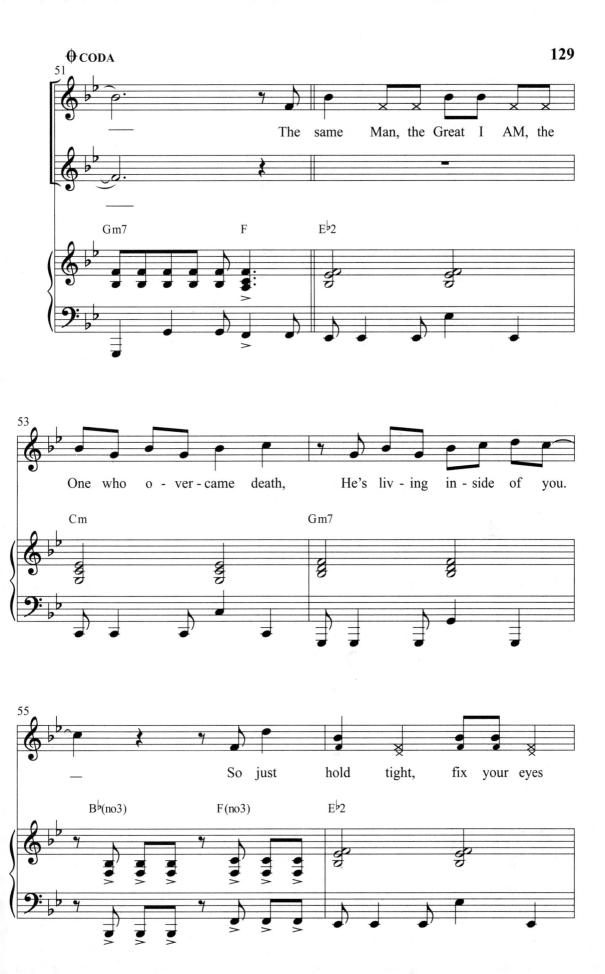

till the fi - nal round. You're not go - in' un -

der 'cause God is hold -

SMALL GROUP

You're not go - in' un - der.

- ing you right now. You might be down

Hold Me

Words and Music by
CHRIS STEVENS, JAMIE GRACE
and TOBY McKEEHAN
Arranged by Brian Hitt

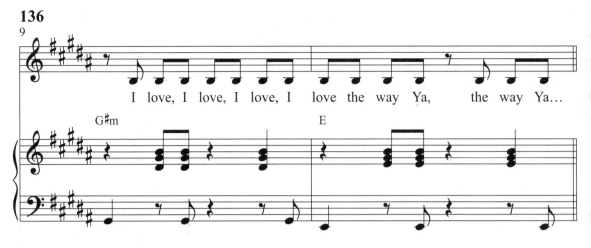

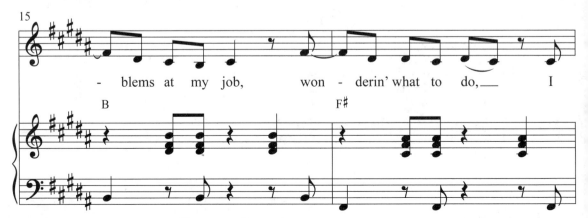

know I should be work-in' but I'm think-in' of You, and

just when I feel this cra-zy world is gon-na bring me down,

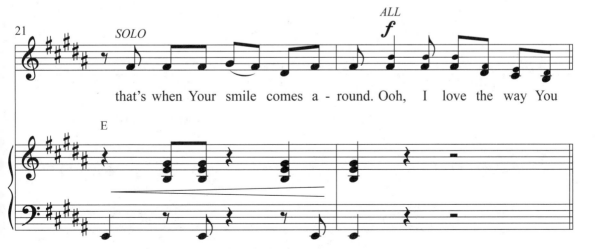

that's when Your smile comes a-round. Ooh, I love the way You

138

146

Good Morning

Words and Music by
MANDISA HUNDLEY, TOBY McKEEHAN,
JAMIE MOORE, AARON RICE
and CARY BARLOWE
Arranged by Brian Hitt

Hel - lo, sun-shine, come what may, I feel some-thin' new in - side me.

ALL

_____ I hear the birds sing-in', now my a-larm's ring-in',

A♭(no3)   B♭sus

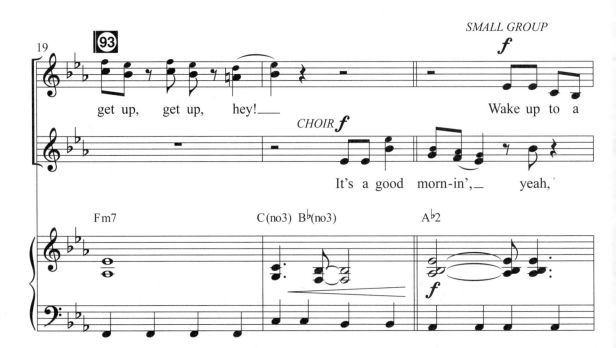

93

get up, get up, hey!_ Wake up to a

SMALL GROUP _f_

CHOIR _f_

It's a good morn-in',_ yeah,

Fm7   C(no3) B♭(no3)   A♭2

oh oh oh oh oh. Oh oh oh oh oh oh oh oh oh oh oh oh.

yeah.

Slow down, breathe in, don't move a - head,__ I'm just

Oh_____ oh_____

liv-in' in this mo - ment. I've got my arms raised, un - fazed,

oh_____ oh_____ oh_____

38 jump out of bed,___ got-ta get this par-ty go - in'.___

oh___ oh___

40 ___ Mmm.___ I went to bed dream-in',

oh.___

A♭(no3)

42 **95** You woke me up sing-in', get up, get up, hey!___

CHOIR

'Cause it's a good

B♭sus F m7 C(no3) B♭(no3)

SMALL GROUP

Wake up to a brand new day,— I've been step-pin',

morn-in', yeah, this morn-in',— yeah.

Ab2   Bb   Cm   Ab2

step-pin' on my way. You give me strength, You give me

Good morn - in',— yeah.

Bb   Cm   Ab2

just what I need. And I can feel the hope that's ris-in' up in me.

It's a good

Bb   Cm   Fm7   Cm7   Bbsus

Oh oh oh oh oh oh oh oh oh oh.

morn - in', ___ yeah, a good

A♭(no3) B♭ Cm

Oh oh oh oh oh oh oh oh oh oh oh.

morn - in', ___ yeah.

A♭(no3) B♭ Cm

ALL

Now, I'm smil-ing, and I'm kiss-ing all my wor-ries good-bye,

Fm Cm

RAPPER ad lib (In the morning, in the morning, in the morning.)
SMALL GROUP

77

Wake up to a brand new day.___ I've been step-pin',

morn-in', yeah, this morn-in',___ yeah.

A♭2   B♭   Cm   A♭2

80

step-pin' on my way. You give me strength, You give me

Good morn - in',___ yeah.

B♭   Cm   A♭2

82   **99** *2nd time*   **1.**   *(page 158, meas. 77)*

just what I need. And I can feel the hope that's ris-in' up in me.

It's a good

1.   *(page 158, meas. 77)*

B♭   Cm   Fm7   Cm7   B♭sus

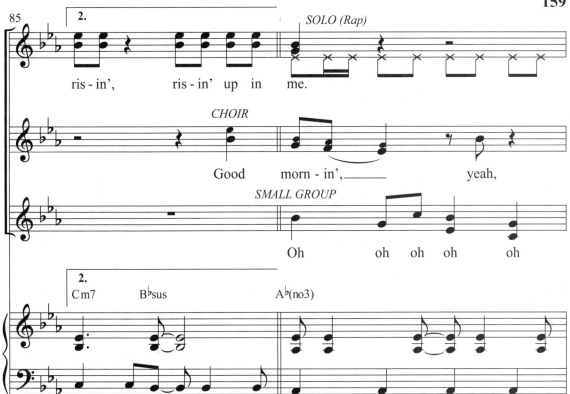